BUILT FOR SUCCESS

THE STORY OF

AT&T

Published by Creative Education and Creative Paperbacks
P.O. Box 227, Mankato, Minnesota 56002
Creative Education and Creative Paperbacks
are imprints of The Creative Company
www.thecreativecompany.us

DESIGN BY **ZENO DESIGN**
PRODUCTION BY **TRAVIS GREEN**
ART DIRECTION BY **RITA MARSHALL**
Printed in Malaysia

PHOTOGRAPHS BY Alamy (Richard Levine; Pictorial Press Ltd,
Frances Roberts; WENN Ltd; World Photo Collection; ZUMA
Press, Inc.), Corbis (Bettmann, Michele Constantini/PhotoAlto,
CORBIS, Kim Kulish, Justin Lane/epa, Reuters), Getty Images
(KAREN BLEIER, Dr. Gilbert H. Grosvenor), Newscom (Leighton
Mark UPI Photo Service, SHAWN THEW/EPA), Wikimedia
Creative Commons (Magnus Manske/Peter Hamer)

LIBRARY OF CONGRESS CATALOGING-IN-PUBLICATION DATA
Murray, Laura K.
The story of AT&T / Laura K. Murray.
p. cm. — (Built for success)
Summary: A look at the origins, leaders, growth, and innova-
tions of AT&T, the telecommunications company that was
founded in 1877 and today provides services to hundreds of
millions of subscribers worldwide.
Includes bibliographical references and index.
ISBN 978-1-60818-556-6 (hardcover)
ISBN 978-1-62832-157-9 (pbk)
1. AT&T (Firm)—Juvenile literature. 2. Telephone companies—
United States—History—Juvenile literature. 3. Telecommuni-
cation—United States—History—Juvenile literature. I. Title.

HE8846.A55M87 2014
384.606'573—dc23   2014028000

CCSS: RI.5.1, 2, 3, 8; RH.6-8.4, 5, 6, 8

First Edition HC 9 8 7 6 5 4 3 2 1
First Edition PBK 9 8 7 6 5 4 3 2 1

BUILT FOR SUCCESS

THE STORY OF

AT&T

LAURA K. MURRAY

A businesswoman reaches her partner on another continent in a matter of seconds. A farmer checks the price of corn from his tractor. A teenager wishes her grandfather a happy birthday over video-chat. In a world that is more connected than ever before, complex networks make it possible to share data and communicate anytime, anywhere. Today, AT&T's data network carries approximately 56 **petabytes** of traffic each day as people send information around the globe. (One petabyte is equal to 13.3 years' worth of high-definition TV.) At one time the world's largest corporation, AT&T helped shape the modern industry of **telecommunications**. But before it connected people on opposite sides of the planet, AT&T connected people who were just down the hall from one another. It was the result of one man's plan to invent the talking telegraph.

CHAPTER ONE

Answering the Call

In 1876, young inventor Alexander Graham Bell said to his assistant, "Mr. Watson, come here, I want to see you!" Thomas Watson heard him and rushed over—from another room. Bell's voice had traveled through his "electrical speech machine."

Three days later, Bell wrote to his parents, "I feel that I have at last struck the solution of a great problem." Still, Bell could not have imagined the impact the device, known as the telephone, would have on the future of the world.

In fact, other inventors had been developing ideas for the telephone for years. But Bell was the first to **patent** his design. Word of the telephone spread across the country as Bell and Watson refined the device. Their research was funded by businessmen Gardiner Greene Hubbard—soon to be Bell's father-in-law—and Thomas Sanders. Hubbard tried to sell the telephone patents to communications giant Western Union Telegraph Company—with no luck. Resolving to go into business for themselves, Bell, Hubbard, and Sanders formed Bell Telephone Company in 1877.

Hubbard acted as the company's president. He decided to lease, or rent, phones to customers instead of selling them. Bell Telephone Company began installing private lines that connected businesses and homes. In January 1878, the United States' first commercial telephone exchange (a network system that connected

Not long after the telephone's invention, Thomas Watson left the business and founded a shipyard.

callers) opened in New Haven, Connecticut. The exchange served 21 customers. Over the next few years, many U.S. cities opened exchanges with Bell licenses. Those exchanges became known as the Bell System.

But Bell Telephone had competition. It hadn't taken long for Western Union to realize its spectacular mistake of turning down the rights to the telephone. Western Union had begun offering its own services to the public using Bell telephones. Its thousands of miles of telegraph wires gave it a head-start in the business. Soon, the outmatched Bell Telephone Company found itself on the verge of **bankruptcy**. It was struggling to find **investors** when Hubbard hired 33-year-old Theodore N. Vail as general **manager**. Vail had been a high-ranking official in the railway mail service, but he believed the telephone was the future of communication.

The forward-thinking Vail proved to be just the leader the company needed. He waged a successful legal battle against Western Union. In 1879, Western Union agreed to leave the telephone business until 1896 and turn over its telephone patents and equipment to the Bell company (which had been recently renamed National Bell Telephone Company). In return, Western Union would receive a royalty, or payment, for every Bell telephone sold. After the deal, investors scrambled to take part in Vail's company. "Bell telephone has a future of fame and fortune in store for it not surpassed by any of the great discoveries of our time," said the *Boston Daily Advertiser*. In 1880, National Bell Telephone Company was reorganized into two companies: American Bell Telephone Company and the Belgium-based International Bell Telephone Company, which would go on to operate in Europe until 1925.

In 1881, American Bell Telephone Company developed the first long-distance network. It stretched from Boston, Massachusetts, to Providence, Rhode Island. American Bell also **acquired** Western Electric Company to make its equipment. Vail next set his sights on improving long-distance service so people could communicate from farther away than ever. To do this, he established the New

Alexander Graham Bell showed government officials—even the Queen of England—how to use the telephone.

York–based American Telephone and Telegraph Company (AT&T) in 1885 and became its president. AT&T was owned by its **parent company**, American Bell Telephone Company.

AT&T's first line connecting New York and Philadelphia could handle just one phone call at a time. But Vail's project grew steadily, even after his 1887 retirement. On December 30, 1899, AT&T acquired its parent company and the Bell System. The new business was called American Telephone and Telegraph Corporation (AT&T). Its long-distance department would become AT&T Long Lines.

By 1905, the Bell System had 2.2 million phones in use. Bell's patents had expired, which created a new age of challenges. Thousands of other companies flooded the market, vying for a place in the budding industry. AT&T found itself in poor financial shape with a reputation for low-level service.

In 1907, a banking group took control of AT&T. Banker J. P. Morgan brought Vail out of retirement. Vail cut prices, created employee benefit programs, and focused on long-term growth. His actions restored AT&T's public image and set the course for its next 70 years of operation. As Vail saw it, the best service would come from having a single telephone provider. And that provider, Vail reasoned, should be AT&T. A national advertising campaign included Vail's well-known **slogan**, "One System, One Policy, Universal Service."

The U.S. government wasn't convinced a single system was best. The Department of Justice worried that AT&T was monopolizing, or controlling, the entire industry. **Antitrust** officials began an investigation. Vail knew there was a chance AT&T could be destroyed. The matter was settled with the Kingsbury Commitment of 1913, a letter from AT&T's vice president Nathan Kingsbury. Kingsbury agreed to a number of conditions, such as allowing other companies to connect to AT&T's network for a fee. AT&T also gave up the controlling **stock** it had recently acquired in Western Union. The commitment included other restrictions as well, but Vail's company was left standing. AT&T had become a monopoly approved by the government.

"All really big discoveries are the results of thought."

ALEXANDER GRAHAM BELL

Influential businessman J. P. Morgan's ventures spanned the railroad, steel, and electrical industries.

1907 Sept. 1

The Bell family, pictured in 1907

ALL IN THE FAMILY

Alexander Graham Bell was always interested in communication and speech. After growing up with a mother who was deaf, Bell became a teacher to those who couldn't hear. He provided children with new ways to communicate and researched the role of vibrations in sound. Through that work, Bell met lawyer Gardiner Greene Hubbard and his daughter, Mabel, who was deaf. Bell and Mabel fell in love, and the inventor redoubled his research efforts to prove himself worthy of marriage. Hubbard helped finance Bell's research and later took on the operations of their telephone company. (Bell was not interested in being a businessman.) Mabel encouraged her future husband to introduce the telephone to the world. Since Bell's invention had earned him the nickname "the father of the telephone," writer Mark Twain once referred to Hubbard as "the father-in-law of the telephone." Hubbard died in 1897.

CHAPTER TWO

A Growing Monopoly

A T&T continued to connect people around the U.S. and then the world throughout the first half of the 1900s. On January 25, 1915, the first official transcontinental (coast-to-coast) line went active as Bell placed a call from New York to Watson in San Francisco. Vail, positioned in Georgia, and U.S. president Woodrow Wilson, sitting in Washington, D.C., also participated in the demonstration.

The line had been years in the making. It was the result of brand-new technology—a type of vacuum tube, which amplified sound—and hours of manual labor by employees who planted telephone poles one by one. The first voice transmission across the Atlantic Ocean took place the same year using radio waves. During this early period in AT&T's history, operators connected all phone calls manually by using a **switchboard** to route the calls through the network. Even though AT&T installed its first dial phones in 1919, the last manual telephone would not be converted until 1978.

In 1919, Vail retired for the second time. He left quite the legacy behind at AT&T. Vail had been responsible for organizing the Bell System into several local Bell

Bell was flanked by AT&T executives as he made the first transcontinental phone call.

Operating Companies (BOCs) under the larger umbrella of AT&T Corporation. He had also expressed the opinion that AT&T needed to develop its own technologies. That vision became reality with the 1925 creation of Bell Telephone Laboratories for equipment design and support and, eventually, research and development.

By this time, there was no doubt AT&T was a global telecommunications giant. In order to describe the extent of the AT&T monopoly, historian John Postley compares the system to a single company owning all cars, roads, and traffic lights. In the early 1930s, U.S. president Franklin D. Roosevelt agreed with other officials that telephone calls between states should be considered acts of commerce, or exchanges of goods. The president signed the Communications Act of 1934. It recognized AT&T as a monopoly but also created a government agency called the Federal Communications Commission (FCC) to regulate the telephone business.

Meanwhile, AT&T's president W. S. Gifford remained focused on the company's ultimate goal: to provide the best phone service at the lowest cost—and to make a **profit** while doing so. With AT&T earning considerably improved reviews since Vail's term, it seemed as though "one policy" was in fact the best. Antitrust officials and potential competitors still weren't happy, but that didn't stop AT&T from becoming one of the world's largest companies. In the 1940s, the company saw its long-distance call volume increase by 350 percent as separated families and friends tried to stay connected during World War II.

By 1945, half of American households had a telephone. Thanks to Bell Labs, those phones were operating faster and more reliably than ever before. In 1941, AT&T had begun installing coaxial cables, the first medium of **broadband** transmission. The cables could carry a higher volume of calls for longer distances than the traditional strung copper wires or underground cables. Six years later, AT&T opened a microwave-relay connection between New York and Boston. It was a lower-cost system in which conversations (and television) traveled by radio waves rather than cables. The technology would continue to play a role in network traffic for decades to come.

London switchboard operators of the 1940s wore steel hats to protect themselves against potential air raids.

Thanks to continuous improvements in **switching** technology, phone calls had become much easier to make. But by 1950, most families still had party-line systems. In a party line, two or more customers shared a telephone circuit. A person could pick up the phone and hear her neighbor, who made calls on the same line. Party lines were a constant source of complaints to AT&T. The system allowed others to eavesdrop or clog up the line with lengthy conversations. Generally, users could upgrade to a more expensive private line, but residents in some rural areas would continue to use party lines into the 21st century.

To keep the growing operation running, AT&T was employing more and more people as operators, technicians, and managers each day. It was also expanding into other modes of communication such as television. In 1927, Bell System had performed the first U.S. demonstration of long-distance television. Live, moving images of U.S. secretary of commerce Herbert Hoover were sent over AT&T's telephone lines from Washington, D.C., to New York. Beginning in 1948, TV networks used AT&T's far-reaching systems to transmit their programs to stations across the U.S. Bell Labs played a key role in AT&T's growth during the early TV era, churning out brilliant technologies such as the transistor (in 1947), a device used to control the flow of electricity. The transistor became an essential part of modern electronics.

In 1956, AT&T's reach into other industries was dealt a blow by the Department of Justice. To settle an antitrust lawsuit and avoid being destroyed, AT&T signed the consent decree of 1956. A consent decree is an agreement that puts an end to a lawsuit. The decree restricted AT&T to its phone services (regulated by the government) and a few government projects. The company was not allowed to expand into other communications industries, such as computing. AT&T was also required to license its patents for such inventions as the transistor to other companies for a fee. The company itself was allowed to remain intact. However, what AT&T **executives** did not realize was that the consent decree would be the first stage in dismantling the largest monopoly in history.

"My first stop on any time-travel expedition would be Bell Labs."

BILL GATES, MICROSOFT COFOUNDER

While Herbert Hoover spoke into a telephone, his TV image appeared to the audience as dots of light.

Dennis Ritchie and Ken Thompson

INVENTING THE FUTURE

AT&T's Bell Laboratories, at one point employing about 25,000, became a global research leader. Its scientists earned seven Nobel Prizes over the years. Among other future-shaping devices, New Jersey–based Bell Labs developed calculators, sound in movies, transistors, solar cells, lasers, and fiber optics. The Labs also had the idea for cellular networks long before the technology existed. Their work paved the way for services such as voicemail, caller ID, and call waiting. "Bell Labs was a mystical institution," recalled George Indig, a patent lawyer for the Labs. "It was the envy of the technological world." In 1969, Bell Labs researchers led by Dennis Ritchie and Ken Thompson developed the Unix operating system, which helped make the Internet a reality. Ritchie also created the C programming language, which is widely used today and serves as the basis for many other programming languages. Modern communications technologies found in devices such as wireless phones are directly descended from Bell Labs.

CHAPTER THREE

The Breakup

On July 10, 1962, NASA launched into orbit AT&T's 170-pound (77.1 kg) *Telstar I*, the first active communications satellite (meaning it amplified and retransmitted signals instead of just reflecting them). As *Telstar* circled Earth, a Bell Labs research team led by Eugene O'Neill used a massive antenna positioned in Andover, Maine, to transmit the first telephone call through space.

AT&T president Frederick Kappel sat in Maine and placed a call through the satellite to U.S. vice president Lyndon B. Johnson in Washington, D.C. Johnson told Kappel his voice was "coming through nicely." The satellite also transmitted the first television pictures across the ocean to ground stations in France and England. The first image relayed from Earth to space and back was of an American flag waving outside the Andover station. *Telstar* marked a new era in communications technology and furthered AT&T's reputation for scientific development.

AT&T might have been the world's largest corporation, but, to some, it was also becoming the most hated. The FCC couldn't keep up with monitoring such a sprawling operation that easily outpaced its smaller, less-connected competitors.

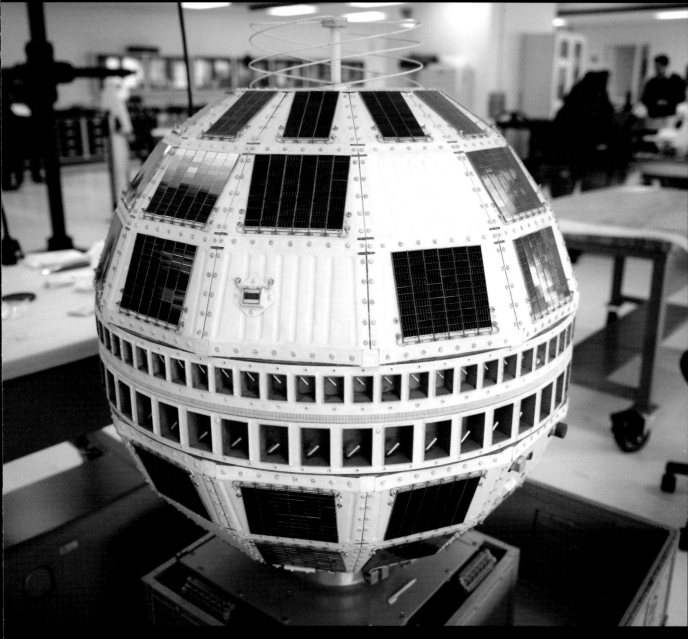

NASA looks back upon the historic launch of *Telstar I* as "the day information went global."

In addition, critics likened AT&T to a long-armed octopus, claiming it was no longer a "natural" monopoly. AT&T's reach was indeed extensive. By 1970, more than
90 percent of American households had telephones, and nearly all the phones
were connected through AT&T systems. AT&T soon found it difficult to keep up
with phone service demand. The company experienced public backlash for the
ensuing slow service and breakdowns. Meanwhile, the FCC was allowing more
competition to creep into the telecommunications industry.

Antitrust officials and rivals such as MCI Communications had kept a close eye on
AT&T's monopoly. AT&T had withstood many lawsuits. But in 1974, the Department
of Justice brought another suit against AT&T, its manufacturing arm Western Electric,
and Bell Laboratories. In a case known as *United States v. AT&T*, the government
accused AT&T's 22 Bell Operating Companies of trying to control markets such as
telecommunications equipment. The government wanted AT&T to free itself of its
BOCs and Western Electric. A lengthy trial finally began on January 15, 1981.

At the time, AT&T was a company earning more than $6 billion each year (but was
burning through hundreds of millions in legal fees). It provided more than one million people with jobs. "No one, outside of the federal government, employs more
human beings," wrote business profiler Sonny Kleinfield in 1981. One observer re-
marked, "[The system] is so big that no one can ever truly understand its immensity."

In 1982, AT&T chief executive officer (CEO) and chairman Charles L. Brown ended
the suit by signing a consent decree. AT&T freed itself of its BOCs, and in exchange,
the government lifted some of the restrictions of the 1956 decree, such as its limits
on AT&T's involvement in other communications industries. In one of the biggest
corporate reorganizations ever, the BOCs became seven separately owned and
operated regional companies. Brown didn't believe the system needed changing,
saying, "I think the nation in the long run will be sorry it happened."

For years, AT&T Corporation had sported the nickname "Ma Bell" as the parent of the Bell System. As of January 1, 1984, the new regional operating companies became known as "Baby Bells." The Baby Bells included Bell Atlantic and US

MCI founder and chairman William McGowan was one of the AT&T monopoly's biggest critics.

West (which later turned into Verizon and CenturyLink respectively) as well as Southwestern Bell. AT&T was allowed to keep its name in addition to Bell Labs and Western Electric. But the Bell System was dead. The newly separated AT&T focused its efforts on long-distance communication, while the Baby Bells charged others (including AT&T) to access their local lines.

By now, AT&T was installing fiber-optic connections, which used pulses of light on glass fibers. Fiber optics cost less and could handle many more calls than electric signals of the past. Despite such advancements in technology, the complex 1984 breakup took a dramatic toll on AT&T's business. Over the next decade, the long-distance services of rivals such as MCI and Sprint grew quickly. AT&T and its competitors dueled over customers who now had more options—and higher expectations. With the dawn of home computers and the Internet, customers began using networks for transmitting data as well as phone calls. To keep up with the transforming industry, AT&T executives dove into other types of communications, acquiring McCaw Cellular Communications for $12.6 billion in 1994.

In 1996, AT&T's stock was down, and its long-distance service was losing customers to competitors. Led by chairman and CEO Robert E. Allen, AT&T underwent a major restructuring. It separated, or spun off, into three independent companies: AT&T, Bell Labs, and a computer manufacturer known as NCR. Bell Labs was renamed Lucent Technologies, and AT&T formed a new research and development division called AT&T Labs. AT&T had a lot of work ahead, as analysts warned that the company needed to make major improvements if it hoped to survive.

As the Telecommunications Act of 1996 (meant to encourage competition within the industry) went into effect, AT&T came up with a plan. The company spent billions on upgrading services, acquiring phone service providers and cable companies such as Tele-Communications, Inc. (TCI) in 1999 and MediaOne in 2000. The company also focused on new media technologies such as broadband Internet service. Unfortunately for AT&T, things were about to take a turn for the worse.

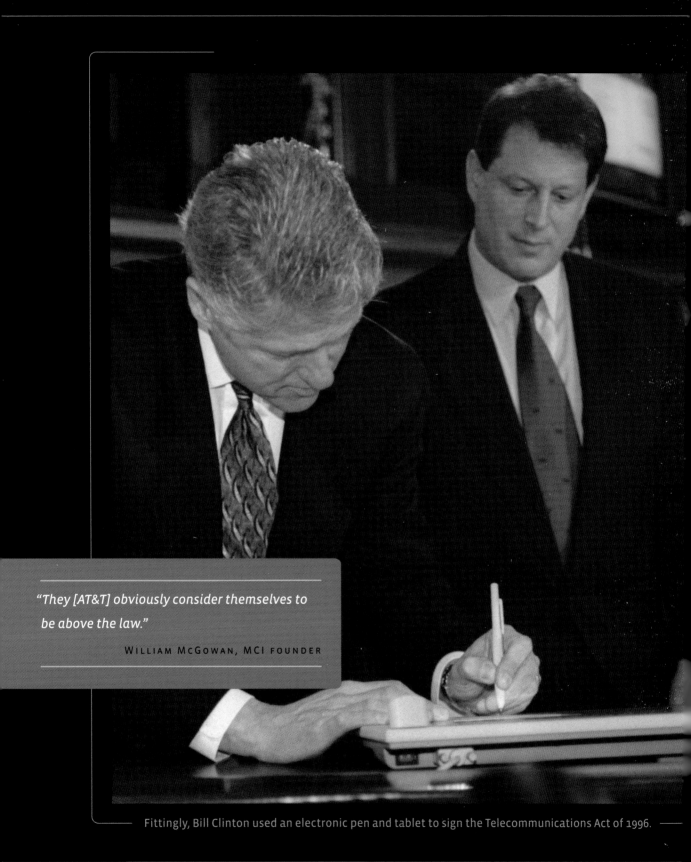

"They [AT&T] obviously consider themselves to be above the law."

WILLIAM McGOWAN, MCI FOUNDER

Fittingly, Bill Clinton used an electronic pen and tablet to sign the Telecommunications Act of 1996.

MAKING THE CALLS

For most of the 1900s, telephone operators were an essential part of making phone calls. The first operators at the Bell Telephone Company were teenage boys, who proved to be too unruly to be trusted with customers. In an effort to present a friendly, polite image, the company decided to hire young, unmarried women for the positions. Besides connecting callers, phone operators became sources for all sorts of information, from news to weather to gossip. They often built friendly relationships with customers and, in rural areas, even performed technological repairs. During its midcentury "Golden Age," AT&T employed more than 350,000 busy operators, nearly all women. But by 1984, the company's operator workforce had shrunk to 40,000 because of the technological advancements that allowed for **automation** and the ability for customers to dial for themselves. Today telephone operators assist mainly in customer service roles.

CHAPTER FOUR

Awaking a Giant

I n 2000, AT&T found itself in **debt** following its bold purchasing spree. Company stock had fallen—and investors were fed up. Chairman and CEO C. Michael Armstrong, who had led AT&T's push into cable TV and Internet services, reminded investors that the recovery process would take time. "I cannot do this in months," he said. "No one can."

Armstrong decided another restructuring was in order. Once again, AT&T created a family of separate companies that this time consisted of AT&T, AT&T Broadband (cable), and AT&T Wireless.

Armstrong believed the specialized companies would earn more **revenue** by focusing only on their particular strengths. AT&T Wireless, operating under the stock symbol "AWE," became an independent company soon after. Its **initial public offering** (IPO) was the largest to date. In late 2002, AT&T Broadband, the nation's biggest cable company, completed a **merger** with Comcast Corporation and began operations under the Comcast name. With the deal's completion, former Baby Bell CEO David W. Dorman took over the leadership of AT&T Corp. He faced multiple challenges, including the telecom crash of 2000 to 2002, a period in which the crowded industry declined, companies failed, and layoffs were widespread.

Chaired by C. Michael Armstrong (left), the newly merged Comcast had more than 21 million subscribers.

By the end of 2004, AT&T was still in a downward slide. At 24 million subscribers, its customer base had shrunk by more than 30 percent over the previous year. Revenue had fallen by 11.6 percent to $30.54 billion, and job cuts numbered in the thousands. "This has been a period of significant challenge and change for the entire telecom industry," Dorman told the *Washington Post* in an article titled "Sun May Finally Be Setting on AT&T." AT&T, however, was about to undergo a historic shake-up—one of the most surprising in company history.

In November 2005, SBC Communications bought AT&T Corp. for $16 billion and also took on the company's $6 billion in debts. SBC had been one of AT&T's own Baby Bells and had changed its name from Southwestern Bell Corporation to SBC. Under the direction of CEO and chairman Edward Whitacre Jr., SBC had enjoyed steady growth. It had quietly bought up companies—including other not-so-little Baby Bells—and acquired a large portion of Cingular Wireless, the country's second-largest wireless provider behind Verizon Wireless. (To make matters more confusing, Cingular had bought AT&T Wireless in 2004.) Although some questioned SBC's decision to take over AT&T Corp., most analysts agreed the acquisition would be in AT&T's best interests. "A deal, for AT&T, makes sense because I really think they would get demolished during the next few years as a stand-alone company," explained market researcher Allan Tumolillo.

Soon, SBC announced that it would take on AT&T's name, which was already recognizable to the public and had a long, respected history. From then on, the business would operate as AT&T Inc. Many called the corporation formed in 2005 "the new AT&T" to set it apart from its past names. SBC also took on AT&T's **branding** and began trading in the stock market under AT&T's longtime symbol "T."

In 2006, the new AT&T, headquartered in San Antonio, Texas, brought in $37.5 billion from wireless services alone, netting a profit of $2.5 billion. In March, AT&T acquired another former Baby Bell called BellSouth. That purchase gave AT&T complete control of the Atlanta-based Cingular, making AT&T the nation's

Texas native Edward Whitacre Jr. served as chairman and CEO of the new AT&T from 2005 to 2007.

largest wireless provider. The same year, AT&T launched a new product. AT&T U-verse offered a combination of Internet Protocol (IP)-based data, video, voice, and wireless services. Unlike traditional cable TV, U-verse TV allowed users to access more channels and digitally record several programs at once. AT&T had built out its fiber-optics network to deliver the new services.

At the same time, AT&T continued to develop its Voice over Internet Protocol (VoIP) services, which were quickly changing the way people used their electronics. VoIP converted a person's voice into a digital signal that traveled through the Internet. The technology allowed people to use services such as Skype to make voice calls through their computers—without paying long-distance rates. Internet-based services were changing the industry in other ways, too. Now, cable companies could offer both voice calling and high speed Internet. They had become the newest serious competitors for phone companies.

Just as Armstrong had predicted, customers were demanding multiple services from their communications providers. Within a few short years, people had come to expect access to many television channels, worldwide cell phone capabilities, video streaming, and lightning-fast Internet. Technology was advancing at a breakneck speed, and customers had their pick of companies. They were going to give their money to the provider offering the best quality at the best price. Future success in the communications industry rested with technology, and AT&T executives knew it. "We're about to become a company with wireless at its heart," Whitacre announced.

But leading the emerging industry wasn't going to be easy, as the field was more crowded than ever. Adding to the congestion was the merger of two prime competitors: Verizon acquired MCI for $8.4 billion at the start of 2006. Soon, Verizon's 56.8 million subscribers pushed it past AT&T's 56.3 million to claim top honors for wireless providers. But AT&T was about to get a big boost, thanks to a man named Steve Jobs.

> "You would say, 'AT&T, this is Rose, how may I help you?' It made it so personal."
>
> ROSE DiMAGGIO TRELA, AT&T PHONE OPERATOR

Verizon Wireless formed in 2000 under the parent company known as Verizon Communications.

In 1889, general superintendent Angus S. Hibbard created AT&T's first logo. Featuring a bell in reference to the Bell System, the image went through several variations, including a 1969 version by celebrated graphic designer Saul Bass. When the Bell System was disbanded in 1984, AT&T Corporation introduced a new logo designed by Bass: a blue globe with white stripes. It represented a world connected by electronic communication. After SBC bought AT&T in 2005, it unveiled a (slightly) modified globe, this one three-dimensional with inverted colors and fewer stripes. Not many people were happy with the new logo that looked so similar to Bass's "beloved" globe. "The third time's not the charm, AT&T," said a *BusinessWeek* article, "and your new blue 'beach ball' is full of hot air." AT&T later added orange to its company colors after acquiring Cingular Wireless in 2006.

CHAPTER FIVE

A Wireless World

On January 9, 2007, Apple CEO Steve Jobs introduced the iPhone at San Francisco's MacWorld Expo. Jobs believed mobile phones would be major contributors to the future of data sharing. He predicted that the multi-touch iPhone, priced between $499 and $599, would revolutionize web browsing.

Then Jobs delivered another big announcement: AT&T would be the sole carrier of the iPhone through 2009. The launch of the iPhone marked a new era in wireless communications—and people would never connect to each other the same way again.

New AT&T CEO and chairman Randall Stephenson, a longtime company executive, had no doubts about partnering with Apple. "This is a once-in-a-lifetime moment to change how the public views AT&T as a wireless company," he said. Stephenson hadn't even seen the iPhone in person when the deal was signed, but he realized the small device would change mobility worldwide. "I don't care if you have to go to every store in America and get a paper bag and paint a globe on it and put it over the signage in each store," he told his team. "We're going to launch this

Steve Jobs's iPhone combined phone, computer, and camera technology in a small device.

under the AT&T brand." The deal paid off. Before the iPhone was released on June 29, thousands camped overnight outside Apple stores to buy their phones. Within 4 months, AT&T's third-**quarter** income had risen by 41 percent, while 40 percent of the 1.1 million iPhone activations represented new subscribers to AT&T's services. Not everything was smooth sailing, though. Many wanted the iPhone to be made available through other providers, and Jobs reportedly thought AT&T was too slow in upgrading its data network.

Stephenson's focus remained on developing AT&T's wireless. Divisions of AT&T that were based on landlines (traditional wire connections) were feeling the industry's shift as well as the bad **economy**. People were disconnecting their landlines— once AT&T's largest market—at a significant rate. Troubles continued as customers expressed widespread dissatisfaction with dropped calls and spotty service. Many analysts believed that the stumbles were inevitable. Since the iPhone's release, AT&T's data traffic had increased by an overwhelming 5,000 percent by late 2009. "Would [the situation] have been different on Verizon?" asked wireless expert Daniel Hays. "Probably not."

Verizon took advantage of its rival's struggles, targeting AT&T (now headquartered in Dallas, Texas) in an ad campaign. Still, AT&T was gaining subscribers. Industry studies showed that AT&T possessed the fastest 3G (third generation) network in the U.S. In 2010, the first full year the iPhone was available on other carriers, the company still saw its revenues from wireless data increase by 28.7 percent. Boosted by the new slogan "Rethink possible," Stephenson focused on connecting new devices such as tablets and e-readers to the AT&T network.

In 2011, Stephenson entered into merger talks with smaller competitor T-Mobile. T-Mobile had built an impressive network, and its parent company was looking to sell. A $39-billion deal would have made AT&T the country's largest cell phone service provider and helped to unclog its busy networks. But some claimed that such a merger would also narrow the field of competition to basically AT&T and Verizon. The FCC declared its disapproval, the Department of Justice sued, and

In 2007, Apple fans waited for hours to ensure they received their iPhone the day it launched.

AT&T withdrew its offer. After regrouping from the failure, Stephenson focused his team on expanding AT&T's 4G LTE wireless network and U-verse broadband service. In 2012, the company reported revenues of $127 billion. That number grew by 1.9 percent the following year.

AT&T continued looking toward the future by reimagining how people could stay connected. It implemented a program in New York City that offered solar mobile charging stations at several outdoor sites. The project was in response to 2012's Hurricane Sandy, a deadly storm that demolished landlines and left millions of East Coast residents without power or means of communication. In 2013, AT&T joined with New York officials and executives from other companies to announce plans for a wireless network in the city's subway system. AT&T also revamped its public image. Its humorous commercials with the tagline, "It's not complicated," featuring candid conversations with children, were a hit among TV viewers. In September, AT&T acquired Alltel Wireless for $780 million. Then, in May 2014, the company made a splash when it announced it planned to buy DirecTV (the biggest satellite provider in the U.S.) for $48.5 billion. The deal would allow the company to offer video through satellites and fiber optics as more people streamed video on mobile devices. But AT&T faced backlash in late 2014 when a government investigation found the company had been unfairly billing mobile customers. AT&T settled for a record $105 million.

In today's many-sided communications industry, AT&T takes the opportunity to partner with other companies and markets. AT&T has made moves to return to its active history of invention by establishing AT&T Foundry tech centers in Texas, California, Georgia, and Israel. In coming years, AT&T plans to work with automakers and farmers who might benefit from mobile services. AT&T also eyed further European expansion. It will need to stay on the cutting edge of VoIP and video. During its long and complicated history, the company that began with one "electrical speech machine" has reformed itself many times over. By continuing to rethink possible, AT&T has the opportunity to shape global communication for years to come.

"We sell very exciting products and services—products and services that change people's lives."

RANDALL STEPHENSON, AT&T CEO

Please do not leave your device unattended. You are solely responsible for any device while charging.

Devices charge at about the same rate as a wall outlet. If your device has a dead battery, please wait 30 seconds for charging to begin.

Visit att.com/attstreetcharge for more information on locations, conversations, and help.

SOLAR POWERED BY

⌀ | GOALZERO

iPhone 5   USB

#ATTStreetCharge

AT&T's free solar charging stations around New York offered ports for various electronics.

CONNECTING PEOPLE

Far from its early days of hiring mainly men as supervisors and women as phone operators, AT&T has gained a reputation for workplace **diversity**. Recently, AT&T has been shown to be a vocal supporter of equal rights. In 2014, AT&T received a perfect score from the Human Rights Campaign, which rates how well businesses treat LGBT employees. In 2013, the company hired more than 3,600 U.S. military veterans, who often already possess skills for careers as technicians. The company planned to double those hiring efforts in the future. As of 2014, around 40 percent of AT&T employees were people of color, while 36 percent were women. AT&T's employees aren't the only ones getting more diverse. In response to the nation's rapidly increasing Hispanic population, AT&T has opened more than 700 bilingual stores. The company also makes sure its **marketing** strategy connects with customers of all backgrounds.

GLOSSARY

acquired purchased another company

antitrust relating to protecting companies from unfair business practices, such as one company gaining total control of a certain market

automation use of machinery or other equipment for tasks

bankruptcy the state of having no money or other valuable belongings, such as property, or being unable to repay debts

branding the name of a product or manufacturer; branding distinguishes a product from similar products made by other manufacturers

broadband a high-speed data transmission that carries a large amount of data at once; common broadband Internet connections include cable and DSL modems

debt money that is owed to a bank or other lender

diversity including people of different backgrounds and ethnicities

economy the system of producing, distributing, and consuming of goods within a society

executives decision-making leaders of a company, such as the president or chief executive officer (CEO)

initial public offering a company's first opportunity for the public to purchase shares of ownership

investors people who buy shares of companies or other organizations in exchange for ownership in that company or organization

manager a person responsible for controlling all or parts of a company's operations

marketing advertising and promoting a product in order to increase sales

merger the combination of two companies into one

parent company an organization that controls management of another company known as its subsidiary

patent earn government-granted rights that allow an individual or company to make, use, or sell specific products or technology

petabyte units of memory size each equal to one quadrillion bytes, or one million gigabytes

profit the amount of money that a business keeps after subtracting expenses from income

quarter one of four three-month intervals that together comprise the financial year

revenue the money earned by a company; another word for income

slogan a short, attention-grabbing phrase used in advertising

stock shared ownership in a company by many people who buy shares, or portions, of stock, hoping the company will make a profit and the stock value will increase

switchboard a panel used to manually connect or control telephone circuits

switching circuit technology used to connect two callers; early telephones involved manual switching by operators

telecommunications communications formed by transmitting a signal over long distances; includes telephone, cable, and broadcast

SELECTED BIBLIOGRAPHY

AT&T Corporation. "Milestones in AT&T Network History." http://www.corp.att.com/history/nethistory/milestones.html.

AT&T Tech Channel. "Party Lines." AT&T Archives. http:// techchannel.att.com/play-video.cfm/2012/6/6/AT&T -Archives-Party-Lines.

Galambos, Louis. "Theodore N. Vail and the Role of Innovation in the Modern Bell System," in "High Technology Industries," special issue, *Business History Review 66*, no.1 (Spring 1992): 95–126.

Gertner, Jon. *The Idea Factory: Bell Labs and the Great Age of American Innovation*. New York: Penguin, 2012.

Guglielmo, Carla. "AT&T's Big Call: Randall Stephenson on the iPhone, His Wireless Ambitions, and the Next Big Thing," *Forbes*, January 2, 2013. http://www.forbes.com/sites /connieguglielmo/2013/01/02/atts-big-call-randall-stephenson -on-the-iphone-his-wireless-ambitions-and-the-next-big-thing/.

Mohammed, Arshad. "Sun May Finally Be Setting on AT&T," *The Washington Post*. October 22, 2005. http://www .washingtonpost.com/wp-dyn/content/article/2005/10/21 /AR2005102102074.html.

Weaver, Robyn M. *Alexander Graham Bell*. San Diego: Lucent, 2000.

Note: Every effort has been made to ensure that any websites listed above were active at the time of publication. However, because of the nature of the Internet, it is impossible to guarantee that these sites will remain active indefinitely or that their contents will not be altered.

INDEX